Killing Silence

Written by
EB Allen

DEDICATION

I would not be who I am today without the love and support of my amazing daughter, CB. All of my dedications will be to her in some way because she is my world and I totally adore everything about her.

CONTENTS

ACKNOWLEDGMENTS

It will sound really weird to thank people who deeply hurt me, but without them I would not be who I am today. SLS, you are completely crazy and I honestly hope that you get help for your stalking issues… but, I owe you a lot for allowing me to see the real man with whom I was trying to build a relationship with. He showed me his true colors when you did all that you did to me. I think the universe put you in our path to stop me from making a huge mistake with him. So, thank you for doing all of that crazy fucked up shit!

And to KS… I am so glad to have met you. Despite all of the crazy drama from your past ruining everything we could have had, you taught me a lot about myself. I really hope you find someone who you can be completely honest with and love for the rest of your life. I hope you stop running away from love, but instead embrace it with your entire being. Continue being your talented self and you will go far. As always, I will think of you ever so briefly whenever I am in Paris.

Love after silence

Sometimes we meet someone that makes us want to fall in love again after years of silence in our life. It causes us to reevaluate the darkness that we have placed ourselves in and makes us want to try to reach out towards the feelings of love. Let love inside and see what happens. It can be a tortuous venture to put your heart out there just to see what happens. You want so badly to have it all work out. You try your best to let the universe have your back, and trust that this is more than just a simple relationship. That is both the joy and the heartache of falling in love with someone. You have such grand hope, but also an overwhelming fear that it will all come crashing down around you in an instant. Sometimes it ends, but sometimes it doesn't. This book is about my journey with meeting someone who I really felt could be the one, but his past crept in with total chaos and led to us ending everything before we really even had a chance to begin. This relationship had a lot of outside drama and ups and downs. I am glad that it all happened because I learned a lot about what I do not want in my life in terms of relationships.

You felt like candy
Sweet and soft
Like the way I remember
Everything tasting at 7
When Halloween faces smeared
And bellies filled
With every piece
Of trick-or-treating sweetness

Speak to me
Without words
Allow us time
To understand
Let me know
How you feel
In the softness
Of every kiss
In the breaths
That you take
By the beating
Of your heart
By the look
In your eyes
Help me
To feel
Safe again

The darkness doesn't stop us
From feeling love
It just makes it harder

Bring Me Home

- love language –
I often speak in a language
No one else can truly understand

Your words feed me
Filling in desires
Long left unsatisfied
A darkness
Waiting to be touched
By the light
That only you
Can satisfy

Bring Me Home

Your eyes told me secrets
Even the ones you had forgotten about
Whispers of past loves and broken hearts
Screamed out as we spoke
Only your words told another story
A happier persuasion
Was it to convince me
Or yourself
Perhaps you need to forget your past loves
And I too will one day be just as forgotten

I rarely open up completely
Mostly hidden away
Is a past that would haunt
Even the bravest of hearts
So I continue to close my eyes
And pretend like you are here
Protecting me from the darkness
Giving me shelter from the storm
Arms that hold me tightly
And lips that kiss me softly
You have always been here
But only in my dreams

The love I have to give
Is solid
But fragile
I can hold onto a ledge
But I prefer
Stable ground

Start something beautiful
With the person you love
Because in the end
Nothing will be the same
Without the love you create
In this universe

Bring Me Home

You left me feeling naked
I am not used to being exposed
By my words
I hide behind the darkness
But you found a way
To shine a light
Directly on my soul

You were like water
Slowly dripping
Down my body
You became a rainstorm
Drenching my soul
Surreal and twisted
You took over
My every thought
Now I dream
Of tasting your lips
Just one more time

Did I shock you
With my heart
Because you
Breathed life
Back into me
With your kisses

Leave me behind
Before you understand
How deep my desires are
Walk away faster
Before you understand
How hard I can love
Walk away

Bring Me Home

She will slip away
From your memories
With each new day
Like a fading photograph
Her edges will blur
Until she is gone
Forever

I wish I had the words
To ease your broken soul
If my arms could hold you
Tight enough to heal
I would never let you go
There is pain
And then there is loss
You will be a loss
That I shall not forget

My mind has been taken over
By thoughts of you
Perhaps I should give in
Satisfy this curiosity
A growing temptation
Masked in the mystery
Of it all

Caught between life
And heart
Watching things
Slowly slipping
Through my fingers
Trying to grasp
Just for a moment
A piece of both worlds
I'm afraid
I'm about to lose everything
All at once

Taking a breath
Deep enough
To take you all in
I would turn blue
Before exhaling you
From my world

Killing Silence

There are things
I want to say
But I remain silent
There are things
I want to
Scream out
Into the night
But still
I remain silent
There are things
I want so badly
But I remain
Silent

Bring Me Home

If I had any chance at all
I would take it
Run away with you
To far off destinations
If I had any chance at all
I would breakdown my walls
Break free from the darkness
Plant flowers
And run wild in the sunshine
If I had any chance at all
I would...

You will soon forget
Everything about me
While I will remember
Every detail
The way you kiss
Your hand on my ass
My hands in your hair
The way you smell
How sweet you tasted
Our last goodbye
Will haunt me
And stay deep inside
Keeping me warm
In this darkness

Bring Me Home

I will write about you
Until the words fail me
I will bleed you out
Onto my pages
Until I have nothing left

His lips were as soft as a summer breeze, gently kissing her cheek. But she wanted a hurricane to pull her in and remind her that she was alive.

Bring Me Home

You don't know me
Not like you should
I will never forget
Your beautiful face
But I am just another girl
Not to be remembered
By you

Killing Silence

There is a secret
Hidden inside your chest
Heard in every heartbeat
Like a rhythm
Of illusions and lies
I should have listened
More carefully

You are the melody
In her heart
That she yearns for
In the middle of the night
You touch her
In all the right places
The ones that make her
Scream out for more
You are the only one
Who gets her
Sweet way of loving

I want more of you
A simple taste
Was not enough
To satisfy
This hunger
Growing deep
Inside of me
Your hands
Those lips
I want
All of you
Wanting all
Of me

Bring Me Home

I shall not compare myself
With a ghost
She is perfect
I am Flawed
There is nothing
More for me
Because you
Will always
Be searching
For her
In everyone
You meet

I believe in love letters written from the heart. I believe that if you feel something powerful for someone, you should tell them and tell them often. I believe in long random conversations in the arms of a lover. I believe that real beauty is on the inside and what is on the outside is not worth dwelling over. I believe that a person can overcome anything bad with the love and support of a good partner. I believe that love can las for as long as you are willing to fight for it. I believe in something that most have lost and that makes me very sad for this world.

Bring Me Home

I want to feel your hands
Slide down my cheek
And onto my shoulders
Your lips following along
Tracing a path
All along my body
I want to feel you
Taking control
Of every part of me

I am wired differently
I feel things too deeply
For most to understand

There is no end
To how much
I adore you
And there is no end
To how badly
I want
To fuck you

Killing Silence

In my heart I feel like you are more
More than just a friend
More than just a fading memory
Of what we once were
In my mind I know that you are not
How do I convince my heart
To let you go forever?

Bring Me Home

I will write
About you
Until I no longer
Feel this way
That might be tomorrow
Or perhaps
I will be 99
And still
Wanting you

It's ok to be confused
It's not ok to drag someone
Through your confusion
You are either both feet forward
At the start of a relationship
Or
You are not

Bring Me Home

I will get over the idea of you
It was simply just an idea
The thought of you and me
It isn't something I want
To get over you
So it will take me some time

I will never be
A fake blonde
Fake tan
Fake nails
Fake personality
Type of person
I am
A complete dork
With nothing more
Than what you see here
I will never become
A barbie girl
To fit in online
Or in the real world

Bring Me Home

Late night walks
Under moonlit skies
Conversations that have no end
Kisses that grow deeper
With every passing moment
A kind and understanding soul
Looking at you like there is
No one else they'd rather be with
Waking up to find
They are still there next to you

Slip into my world
Let the night
Take us
Beyond this existence
Forget about time
And let your
Body become
Part of mine

Bring Me Home

I want honesty
No matter how painful
I desire an understanding
Of how anyone can lie
Even when the truth
Is so obvious
And hard to hide
You still choose
Lies

You left a mark on my skin
And a sweet taste
Deep in my mouth
Impossible to forget
No matter how hard I try
Now there is a wanting of more
Than just a simple taste

I am tangled up
Inside a web of
Desires and fantasy
Never knowing
Which is real

It is the fullness of your hands
As they caress my skin
And the weight of your body
As you lay on top of me
And take control
It is also the sweetness in your kiss
All of that reminds me of
Running naked
In the hot summer air
Hoping to not get caught
As we jump wildly into the water

Bring Me Home

It's going to hurt
Not knowing you anymore
People always say they will keep up
Not sure why that lie carries weight
No one ever keeps up when they leave
And those voids sometimes never get filled

I gave you a loaded gun
Pointed straight at my heart
Is it alright dear
If I pull the trigger
Is it alright if I bleed out
All of my sins here before you
Is it alright dear if I die now
Laying here in your arms
For I cannot survive you
Not this time around

I became so lost
In a world I created
To save myself from heartache
That I forgot what it was like
To feel loved
By someone sweet and kind

I feel this need
To be as beautiful
As you see me
I feel this desire
To touch your heart
And know you better
I feel this anticipation
For all of your flesh
To be entangled with mine

I would ask you to stay
If I thought you would
I would hold you all night long
If I thought it mattered
I would kiss you deeper
If I thought you could feel it
I would fuck you often
If I thought that would keep you
I would save you from your pain
If I thought you wanted that

There is something real
About the way this feels
And yet
I cannot let myself believe
Because I have been living
In a silence for too long
The kind that captures your soul
And holds on tighter than anything
Or perhaps I am still dreaming
The way you seem to settle
Deep inside me like a fantasy
Yes, this must be all a dream

Melancholy vibes is what the middle of the night feels like
without you here beside me. Someone to whisper sweet nothings
in my ear and remind me what love feels like.

Sometimes you must let go
Before you even had a chance
To hold on
Sometimes what you want
And what you can have
Are not the same
This is one of those times

Bring Me Home

I will take you in my arms
And love you until the morning light
For you are the only one
I want to see each night
And for all the mornings after
Everything in between the dark and the light
Is for us to discover
And for no one else to understand

It often escapes me
This feel of
Something deep down
In my bones
Being off
But not being able to see it
Not clearly anyway
One day I will understand
But for tonight
I will accept the unknown
And venture forward
Despite the outcome
I fear that awaits me

There is no comparing a love loss
Some lose their entire world
While others lose merely a fantasy
That was never real to begin with
Both can hurt
But the loss is not equal

Is it the beauty of your soul
Which grabs hold gently
Like a warm summer breeze
That touches the skin
And continues to wrap all around
As you carry on about the day
Leaving a happy smile deep inside me

Bring Me Home

Everything changes in life
Even people
You cannot expect the same today
As you did yesterday
You have to flow with it
And grow with people
If you want to keep them around
Or get used to saying goodbye

I have written so many things that I will never post. I have poured my soul out but it is not worthy of view. No words can quite do justice for how I feel so I will bleed out onto a thousand pages and then burn them when I'm done.

I keep getting lost
In these moments
Little pieces of time
Where I think
Only about you
Your sweet kisses
And everything else
All mixed into
A vivid
Yet surreal
Daydream

I would love to show you
A world safe from the darkness
Just laying here in my arms
I would love to give you
Everything you want
Just laying here loving each other
I would love to be the one...
But I am not the one
You dream about in the night

Bring Me Home

You grabbed a piece of my soul
When you slapped my ass
You touched my heart
With every bite on my lip
You twisted my mind
When you rested on my chest
You are a sweet evil
Something I had been missing
In my life

If I had any chance at all
I would take it
Run away with you
To far off destinations
If I had any chance at all
I would breakdown my walls
Break free from the darkness
Plant flowers
And run wild in the sunshine
If I had any chance at all
I would

It would be foolish of me
To think more
Than before
Or less than now
Then again
I am a fool
For believing a feeling

I will always be living in the shadow
Of that girl you really dream about
I will never compare
With her fake blonde hair
And adorable crooked eyes
Sometimes you learn more than you wanted
From what you see
Creeping into your online world

Bring Me Home

His eyes cried out
A wanting of something
Deeper than this
Whatever this is
So I took a chance
And let you inside
Further than anyone before
Please do not disappoint me

I can take the pain
And disappointment
Once again
You are not the first
To let me down
So easily
And you will not be the last
To blind me with a pretty face
And lies told behind cold eyes

Bring Me Home

It's not personal
Letting go
Of someone barely known
A selfish escape
From the darkness
You would have surely
Brought about
To my fragile world

I am in awe of you
I want to lay back
And watch you work
Your mind
Is perfectly beautiful
And I want to live
Inside your world
Even for just today

I am really good at saying fuck
And making silly faces
Instead of serious ones in photographs
I cannot imagine not being
Completely sarcastic
When I am nervous
Somehow all of that fades
When I am with you

I have washed it twice
But damn
It still smells like you
I have taken so many
Deep breaths wearing it today
Just trying to remember
Everything about you
All I have left now
Is my favorite shirt
With a fading scent

Do not bleed out
Your past loves
Onto your present loves
They deserve more
Better
Than to become stuck
In your past
With you
Move forward together
Or alone
It's always your choice
To let go
Or to
Hold on tighter
To your past

Her arms will wrap around your entire body and begin to heal what is broken inside your tired soul. With her kisses she will bring your world new life. Her love will transform you into something you never thought was possible… to feel like you are really living. And for the first time in your life you will forget about death and focus only on her.

Bring Me Home

There are no wrong roads
To finding love
The universe has fought
To get you
Exactly where you are
If you are open
To letting
Someone in
Let it happen

There is a moment when you catch yourself looking at someone and wondering what, if anything, is possible. You stop yourself from falling into something deeper than that moment because it is just simply a moment. Yet life is just a sequence of millions of moments leading up to this one particular moment. Perhaps you were meant to be there all along. Maybe you should let yourself feel it for all that it is and let go of your fears. Then again... it is probably just a passing moment in time.

Your lips are a sweet treat for my soul. They become mixed up with mine and I can no longer understand anything about myself or the universe. Then your hands begin to touch my skin and I am no longer in my own world. All the darkness slips away from me until I am completely lost in your world.

The fact that I can get so lost in your eyes when my mind typically focuses on something until it devours my soul... that is the best feeling in the world; being so lost in you. I owe you more than I can ever repay and all you are doing is simply being there for me when I need you the most.

Just lay here with me for tonight. Let me feel your heartbeat beneath my head. No words are needed. Just wrap your arms around me until we both fall asleep. I need to escape the world for just a little while longer. You are my sweetest escape and I wouldn't have it any other way.

I should be happy, but I cannot help but feel this indescribable pain tugging at me from my soul. I want so badly to feel as if nothing is wrong, but I cannot. I see you but I feel like you see through me as if you are looking at another person somewhere else. I am not going to deny that I like you, but I feel like you do not have any interest in me beyond sex. That makes me want to run away. Fast.

I shall deny myself the heartache that comes from loving you. I will hold back every feeling that leads to you. There shall not be a time of those three words being uttered. Not by me anyway. You can have any part of my body but my heart will remain guarded until I know it's safe to come out again.

- His beautiful lightbulb photo -
The light spirals in beautiful patterns
Illuminating the darkness within
Flecks of colors bounce off
In hues of blues and orange
Oh, but that red
It's the red that draws you in
Like a heart beating
Just for you

April, 27, 2019

I feel like I have been accused of murder. Someone made up a horrible story and vicious lie about me. Told it to someone I cared deeply about. I could spend the rest of my life trying to convince them that it wasn't me. In the end it doesn't matter if they believe me, the damage that person created is already done. They win with a lie and I lose with the truth. I am not a fighter. I just want peace in my life. This is destroying me inside and I cannot do anything about it.

She holds on
Waiting for you
To come back
Into her life
Part of you
Still wants her too
I am but a bystander
In a distant romance
Thinking I was
Something more to you
When I was actually
Second best

I would fight for love
But only if it would fight for me too
I would die for love
If it would kill for me
I want a love worthy of it all
But only if it is willing
To risk everything
For me

You hurt me deeply
Believing her lies
Over my truth
You cannot take back
Things that you said
Nor the feelings I felt
I was into you
Now I cannot see
Past this hurt
Caused by you

Fuck.

What the fuck am I doing?

You kiss me and I want everything about you to become a part of me. You touch my skin and there is nothing stopping me from devouring you in my mind. I hold back as much as I can in reality, but I am only human so I give into the desires. You drive me completely crazy with just a little look. In my heart, I know that I should just run away from you, because this will eventually end badly for me.

No one every stays.

My mind is racing with questions. What if you are the one I have been looking for? What if you do not feel the same way? What if you do feel the same way? What if we made each other happy and didn't want for anything else? What if you are still here with me when I wake up every morning? I think I want more than now and my mind is wanting you to feel that way too.

Bring Me Home

We are among the forgotten
Strung about by ex-lovers
A little bit lost inside
Yet, still worthy
Of being loved by many
Or perhaps even just a rare few
Those worthy enough
To take on a broken heart
And kiss it all better

If you pretend your heart isn't there
Then what the fuck are you living for?
Just let me know what you want
I'm not running away
Not just yet anyway
Come closer to me
Let me listen to your heart
Give me everything you've got
I'm not afraid

Bring Me Home

You'll never understand
This view I have
Looking right at you
Amazing and beautiful
Perfect and sweet
You can never feel
The warmth of your flesh
As you close in on me
Kissing me deeper
And sweeter
Every single time

There is a beautiful light
Calling out my name
From just beyond the darkness
It is sweet and soft
As it gently flows through my veins
I beg it to come even closer
To meet me in the darkness
Because the only thing I know
The thing keeping me safe right now
Is this darkness

Bring Me Home

It is a brutal softness
The way you leave me wanting more
Every time we part

I want someone who wakes up wanting to talk to me
And lets me know they miss me whenever they miss me
I want someone who gets in bed at night
And misses me so much they call to tell me
I want someone who wants me so badly
They feel like losing me would be an actual loss to them
I want someone who kisses me with passion
And fucks me like they want to fuck me forever
I want to feel their love for me
Even if we are simply holding hands watching a movie
I want to be loved... I just want to be deeply loved

A room is just four walls until you find yourself lying there next to someone you want to be with. Then it becomes a place filled with memories and emotions. Each crack on the ceiling can recall a night spent in bed. The shadows on the walls dance and flow with each breath. You become a part of it. And you soon realize that the walls speak of others who have been there before you. The crack is no longer just a crack but a history of many other lives. And you suddenly feel small and insignificant about your tiny moment in that room. Perhaps you should just let go of the walls and set yourself free.

I've been drinking you down
Taking you all in
As if I want to drown
Deep into the abyss
That is your soul
Deeper inside you
With each new breath
I dive into the unknown
Willingly

Bring Me Home

Haunt me once again
With you deep kisses
I miss the way you made me feel
Scattered and torn apart
Searching for you heart
And with nothing left to lose
Except the darkness
That holds me dearly
Just out of reach
Of your loving arms

I want something
More than just this
Whisper of a relationship
I want something more
Kisses that are deeper
With each escaping breath
I want something more
To feel your love inside
My quickly beating heart
I want something more
Than I have ever had before
From you or anyone else
I want... no, I deserve something
More than just this

Bring Me Home

Take these doubts and demons
Toss them out with the garbage
As you tell me I am not the one
Not the one you are looking for
I am what everyone is looking for
A sarcastic personality
With a body to match
And a sly grin
To knock you on your ass
Just before I rip off
All your clothes
And devour your flesh
With you diving deeper inside me
Each and every hour of the night
Don't tell me I'm not enough
Because I'm fucking more
More than you can ever handle
In your tiny little existence
That you claim is everything
When it is I who is everything
And you who is not

I am weak for you
Right before falling asleep
Happily in your arms
I want to tell you
How deep my heart goes
As it pulls me into the abyss
Of wanting to love you
Drowning in a spiraling tidal wave
Of emotions of wanting you
To be someone more than this
Just a simple good fuck
That is turning into a desire
Of wanting to know you more
Beyond the sweaty flesh
And deep kisses
As we lay holding hands
I wonder if you too are thinking
This could be more
Or if your mind wanders off
To another girl or another time
Somewhere far away from me
These thoughts are growing
Stronger by the day
And the not knowing
Is starting to kill me
Just a little bit more each day

Why do I torture myself
With these thoughts of you
They are never more than that
Just empty dreams of wanting
To be next to you every morning
But in reality there is the walk
The shameful walk
At 6:00 am as I hustle out your door
Making my way home to clean up
Washing away smells of sex and your sweat
From every inch that you touched
Taking my time to recall each moment
Your hands touched my skin
And the deep kisses on my neck
But I fear that is all this is for you
Just a hot night spent in bed

Your words are sweet
And your kisses even sweeter
They pull me deep into you
As our clothes hit the floor
And you pick me up onto the bed
I try to push everything else out
Of my mind and into the darkness
But the hiding and the lies
The pain and the hurt
Your past and my future
All tangled up together
In a huge knot of chaos
That screams deep inside me
Telling me to run away
To never look back
But your words are so sweet
And your kisses even sweeter
I once again fall into your arms
And one night becomes another
Then another night of passion
Takes me to a place
That i can no longer run from
A realization that my heart
Has begun to feel more than it should
For someone who has no desire
To feel anything more for me
Than my flesh against his

Bring Me Home

Why her?
Is it the way she speaks to you
The way she makes you feel inside
Does she give you something I cannot
Or is it simply her looks
That keep you running back for more
Because I cannot see past her crazy
That she brought into my life
I can only see the hurt and destruction
She may have a nice face
But her heart is clearly tainted
With hate and lies
Her mind is clearly made up of deceptions
That you are unable to see
Today I am torn between staying and leaving
I cannot imagine a world with your still adoring her
And my being still in it
There is no place for someone new
If you are stuck holding onto the old

I hurt for moments when I realize that I need to say goodbye to you. Then my mind settles and I understand that if you actually wanted to be in my life you would have not believed her lies over my truth. You would have not ran back to her so easily after the chaos she created. You cannot see it now, but maybe one day you will look back and see that you could have had it all with me. Instead, we are soon to be strangers. We were nothing more than a tiny blip in the lives we will continue to live apart from each other. I hope that she is worth it. The friendship that she provides to you. I am a rare individual, and you will never meet anyone like me ever again.

I am not like most girls. Heck, I am not like most humans. I cannot explain myself completely because I am just the way I am inside and I will never change. I feel things deeply, but I can also push aside my feelings and move forward without letting the pain and emotion cause too much damage to my mind. I care for people forever and that haunts me greatly in many circumstances. I want people to live their lives and be happy… even if that never includes me again. My main goal in life is to see people happy with who they ultimately become. I want to find someone to love me, because I have a lot of love to give. I am not willing to settle just to have love enter my life. I deserve to have someone who can equally match me in the love department. I will find it in someone and life will be amazing.

You must always understand that you alone are enough. Having a boyfriend, girlfriend, husband, fiancé, or partner does not complete you. You are amazing and beautiful all on your own. You can and will accomplish great things. Having someone else to share things with is a wonderful part of life, but not having someone is not the end of your beautiful world.

There is an emotional wreckage that takes over when you see the person you are trying to love interacting with their ex. You try not to go there, because that is not your business. Not really. He is his own persona and is allowed to keep up with anyone that he wants. But you cannot help it. Your heart sinks and your mind goes places that it normally would not go.

I cannot fight my own heart
From wanting to be more
With you
I will not dwell on the pain
That comes with not knowing
If you will ever feel the same
About me

Bring Me Home

You asked me to open up
So I did
You got so upset with my words
As I explained your crazy ex
And all the things she had done
You were more concerned with her
Than you were with me
Why did she do those things
You kept asking out loud
I felt you pulling away from me
With each passing minute
You drove away upset
Refusing to speak with me
Despite my opening up
You closed down
And I cannot accept that
As an answer to us
Ever being anything more
Because I need so much more
Than a closed car door

Killing Silence

You have remained silent
Days have gone by now
Without a single word
Two months into this
And you vanish
Over something so simple
I need a strength of character
That will withstand the chaos
And let me in
When things go sideways
I need words to fill my mind
Before all of this silence
Drags me away
Never to be seen again

Bring Me Home

I am falling behind my breath
Holding it in for longer and longer
Before letting it go
Escaping in the tiny moment
Just before it escapes my chest
Wishing so badly that it would vanish
That I would vanish along with it
For just that tiny moment
I want to hide myself away
From all that is killing me today
There are no answers to the pain
Holding it all in and wanting to escape

I buried the thoughts of you
Deeper than before
Not deep enough it seems
I wanted to end myself
Bury my soul to forget
That you had even been here
Cut my flesh wide open
Everywhere you had touched
Bite off my own lips
To forget your kisses
I wanted to end me
To avoid all of the pain
I wanted to end it
All of it

Bring Me Home

You were perfect for me
But so very wrong
I wanted all of you
You wanted none of me
There were warning signs
I ignored every one of them
You kept me entranced
I was drunk on your kiss
There were warnings
I was an addict
You were a drug I needed
So desperately
Strung out on you
I wanted to end me
I twisted the knife
Into my own soul
Walking away
To save my own life

Killing Silence

I could hear it
Deep in your soul
Echoing across my skin
With every kiss
You left scars
Cutting me open

Bring Me Home

Is this just what happens
When I want for more
The universe tricks me
Into feeling everything at once
And then takes everything
That I grew to love
Dragging me back
Into the darkness
Where I guess I must belong
Alone

I cannot find the words
Buried deep inside my head
Where the monsters frolic
And demons gather
Just to keep me sane
For another day
Of this silence

I was so ready for the idea of love
It fell into me so quickly with you
The idea of wanting ore with you
But I was so blinded by the idea
I forgot to see things clearly
When the chaos was hitting me
Right in the face
I chose to ignore everything
I simply wanted to get lost
In loving someone

This silence is painful
You have closed off
From my world
Without a care
Of my feelings
Without understanding
Of my pain
Which is in itself
The answer
To my biggest question
Do you even care
About me?

Bring Me Home

It seems a distant dream
This illusion of love
I try to capture it
Hold it deep inside
Yet it escapes me
Once again
I wanted you
To be the one
To fill my world
With your love
But it escapes me
Once again

I hold onto this fantasy
Of your beautiful lips
Kissing me deeply
Your strong hands
Holding me tightly
I hold onto this dream
Of your heart
Loving me
Deeper each day
I will hold onto
Dreams ad fantasies
Because I no longer
Have you

Lost in the distance of your voice
So far away from yesterday
When I thought I would hear it again
Before you said goodbye

I cannot cry for you forever. I must pull myself back up and remember that I am amazing on my own. Tears clean the soul and they allow us to heal from all that breaks us. You broke my heart. I will recover but for today, the tears will flow down my face. They will remind me of you and what we almost had together.

Bring Me Home

I am not a fragile soul
True you can hurt me deeply
But first you must defeat me
And that my friend...
Is not an easy task
For my armor is solid
And I yield a weapon
Unlike anything seen
On this earth before

It will always be more important for me that you find happiness in life than to stay with me. If I do not make you happy enough to stay... then please go find your happiness out there in the big beautiful world. You are more than just someone to love to me... you are an individual who deserves respect and acknowledgement of what you need and desire. I will never force anyone to stay in my life. I just want everyone to find what truly makes their heart sing. Even if that is not me.

I just want to adore you
In the dorkiest way possible

I will hold onto your pain
As if it were my own
I will take away your stress
With all that I have
I will love your broken heart
With my loving heart
I will give you my everything
If you will let me

The thing about saying "*maybe in another life we will get it right...*" about someone you loved is that the universe knew you were wrong for each other in this life. It will probably know who is best for you in the next life too. Don't attach yourself in the next life to someone from this life. Let yourself find happiness and love naturally and trust that you will find the right person... no matter what life you are living.

Today I am struggling
With the memory of you
I am feeling lonely
But not just a normal lonely
The kind you feel in your soul
Because it wants to reach out
Reach for the lost touch
Something I felt so deeply
But it has gone away
I am missing you today
And that is killing me inside

Bring Me Home

Feeling stuck
In the in-between
Where I still want you
But having to let you go

I have pulled the dagger
From my beating heart
Wiped its blade
And kept it for a treasure
You may have wounded me
But I will continue to battle
For the prize of loving someone
Is always worth the scars

Bring Me Home

I will bury myself
Deep inside this silence
Let it eat away
At my flesh and bones
Until nothing is left
But a loving soul

I have set free my darkness
Unleased the demons
Awakened the ghosts
And I am still here
Still missing you
Still wanting you
Still bleeding
From the wounds
You left behind

Count me down
Lose track of time
Hands in hair
Lips on skin
Bodies as one
3 2 1
Counting down
Until we say goodbye
Once again

You keep your heart locked up
In a prison of your own making
No one can ever truly love you
Because you will never give your heart
You are afraid to be loved
You are lonely, but fulfilled by desires
Only of the flesh by your choosing
I would have loved you behind the prison walls
Where you lock yourself away at night
If you would have let me in
I would have proved your theories about love
To be completely wrong

Bring Me Home

You pulled me under
No air beneath the water's edge
I see everything so clearly
Through the ice above me
I punch until my hands bleed
Destroying my entire body
Just to try to escape this pain
No more air to breathe
Destroying myself from the inside out
Desperate for a hand to grab me
Desperate for a heart to love me
Desperate for an escape from this hell
So tired of bleeding out my soul
For people who would sell it for another

Killing Silence

Your words sink inside me
I crave more
I desire your touch
A longing to feel your words
Slowly drifting inside my ear
As your hands softly touch me

Bring Me Home

You were never meant to be my love
You were pure lust
Love doesn't struggle to speak
It opens up every part
Even the darkest corners
They open up for love
Lust covers up
And runs away
When things get too rough

The heart breaks for the wrong ones just as it does the right ones. Letting go of someone you let inside your world is never easy.

My heart sinks
Deeper
I struggle
Fighting for air
Surviving
A day
And another
Reaching
For a hand
A heart
Anything
Save me
From this
Hell

I was so afraid of losing you
That I held myself inside
I was so afraid to speak to you
That I held myself inside
I was so afraid of angering you
That I held myself inside

I set myself free from fear
You walked away from me
I set myself free from holding my tongue
You walked away from me
I set myself free from your anger
You walked away from me

*I set myself free from you

One day I will find someone who wants to be loved by me, and that will be the luckiest person alive, because my love isn't like any other love.

I've been down this dark path before and clawed my way back. I will find my way out again…

I am the darkness that consumes me.

Fighting for peace of mind requires a weapon I put down a long time ago. It will take me some time to forge a new one in the fires that are burning down my world.

I am breaking. Parts of me that I never even knew existed are being destroyed. I will rebuild, just not today.

I am not sorry for feeling something for you. I am not sorry for letting you in. I am not sorry for all of the pain she caused me. I am not sorry for all of this hurting. I am only sorry for not being enough for you. I wish I was so much more... but I am not.

I believed in magic once. I believed in fairytale endings. I believed in love. I believed in you.

I believe in pain. I believe in darkness. I believe in heartache. I believe in no one.

It is a sweet pain that rips my heart open whenever I think about you.

You stained my blood with your touch. I will forever bleed you
out as a poems to try and heal my broken soul.

.

I am destroyed by an idea of someone, but not that actual someone. This pain is all because of my desires to have something that doesn't exist. Real love. Future plans of me being a certain type of person. This pain I feel is on me, not you.

Lover, lover
I've been thinking
About the prison
Where you keep your heart
I would break you out
If you weren't so criminal
In your thinking about love
You lost the key to your heart
Long ago
You prefer the prison cell
Than a chance at being loved
By a heart like mine

I will defend my heart. Keep it safe from those who cannot feel love. Only those who are capable of love shall know my true name when my heart whispers it in their ear. Until that day, you can never truly hurt me... because you do not even know me.

I will write about you until the pain stops. Then I will write about you until my last breath. You are worth all of the words my soul spills out.

I want to be remembered by the ones I loved.

The tip of my tongue still misses the way you taste.

You think I deserve better, I think I deserve you.

I never had a chance to kiss him goodbye. Ghosts like that never go away.

I would walk through hell
For you my love
My veins would rip open
And bleed out all of your sins
To protect your heart
From the weight of the world
That clearly rests upon you
I would burn to ashes
And rise again like phoenix
Just to keep you safe
For you my love
I would do anything

My wish for you is real love. Not just someone to fill a temporary void for a short time. I want you to find someone that makes you feel. Really feel deep in your soul. Someone that makes your heart fill with joy just by sitting quietly next to you. That person who knows everything about you and you know everything about them. Someone you wake up wanting to text good morning. Not someone you text at 2:00 in the afternoon because you happen to remember you are dating them. I want you to find someone that makes you want a relationship to last forever because everyone deserves to find that person. I want all of that for you.

I will be touched deeply again
But not in the same way
I will dive into loving someone again
But it will never feel the same

Because you changed my heart
In all of the best ways possible

Love is the hardest and the easiest thing to give someone.

Maybe if I cut deeper the blood will write a different story than the ink.

Be silent
Pull me into
Your darkness
Let me kiss away
Your demons

The echoes of your touch still send vibrations down my body and into my soul.

I have visible scars on my flesh, deep rooted scars in my mind, bloody scars on my soul, and a very broken and tattered heart... this is why I love people so deeply when I love. I have been through hell and I do not want anyone to ever feel that lost.

You made me believe I was worth something, and then you made me feel worthless.

Love should send fucking shivers into your soul.

Between the beats of my heart
My soul screams out
Desires go unmet
Wanting to be touched
By another loving soul

The way you left my world will always haunt me.

Smart women never force a man to see their amazing qualities. They continue to be amazing for the men who do notice and they do not worry about the rest.

I have untangled the mess you created inside my soul. I can breathe freely once again.

Sweet lips
Sweet kisses
Sweet eyes
Sweet body
Sweet sex
Sweet soul

Chaotic mind
Chaotic heart
Chaotic past

You never did add up perfectly, but I liked you despite the bad math.

I used to trust words just a little bit more. Until I met you. Now I am not so sure. If a sweet mouth like yours could tell such sadistic lies… then my heart doesn't stand a chance.

If I opened up your soul, even just a little bit, then our time together was worth all of the pain of when you said goodbye.

Bring Me Home

Kiss me deeply
Fuck me deeper
But stay
Stay

I dream and everything to me all at the same time. Making getting over you confusing as fuck.

Your narcissistic boy charms will work on many girls. I am no longer one of them.

We will never become what I had hoped for us. Now I hope for better.

My tears feel heavy on my sun kissed cheeks. Like their weight will erase my existence… or somehow punish me in a million other ways for allowing you to hurt me so deeply.

If you stay today
I will kiss you
If you stay tomorrow
I will fuck you
If you stay longer
I will love you
If you stay forever
I will let you into my secret world

* but you have to stay

Some silences feel almost violent as they destroy our hearts and minds.

Killing Silence

There are days of silence
Where I am left searching
For a meaning behind it
Gaps of language
Drive apart souls
To the point of destruction
Speak often with love
Or leave me be

Bring Me Home

I reach for you in my dreams
And I try to imagine
A world with you here
Every day
Every breath
Every night

I will fight the darkness today and I will cry one last time. For you are now buried somewhere deep inside my heart shaped box of misfit lovers. I buried you under all the rest, because your ghost has been the loudest.

The hardest people to let go of are the ones we thought had more potential to be more in lie. Not just in love but in life. Those we wanted to help reach their full potential.

Your silence is the loudest answer of them all.

Bring Me Home

I should have known you were just a player
When you sent me a sexy shirtless photo of yourself
You sent it to me on April 10, 2019
But it was geo-tag dated January 16, 2019 at 12:05 am
Long before I had even met you
You sent this photo to another girl
Sure you looked sexy with your "*come and get me*" eyes
But it was not meant for me, but for another
Recycled photos from a used up man
Too narcissistic to understand

I am fine until I hear your name
It isn't even your name
Just a name of a coworker
Then it hits me again
You left without trying
People call him Brian now
Jokingly for another reason
I still know his real name
Same as yours
Same pain
Same sadness
Same ending

Bring Me Home

Once my lover
Briefly my friend
Now you are nothing
You pushed your way into my life
Said all those sweet things
Treated me like I was special
We fucked, and fucked
And we fucked some more
Your crazy ex pulled shit
She kept pulling shit
You took her side
You kept believing her crazy lies
She kept on being crazy towards me
You closed off from me because of her
You then said "let's just be friends"
You didn't want to be friends
You just wanted someone to fuck
Someone to easily walk away from
When things didn't go your way
You became the monster
We tell our daughters about
Watch out for liars and thieves
We tell them regularly as a warning
Those monsters will lie to get you into bed
They will steal your heart away
Say such sweet things to confuse you
They walk away quickly
They never look back again
Just like you did with me

You called me babe
Before you ever called me by name
Maybe it is easier to remember
Or perhaps easier to forget
All of the girls in your life
If they are all called *babe* inside your head
I tried to have meaningful conversations
But you would say, *"awe babe, you're cute"*
Then you would deeply kiss me
Filling my mouth with your tongue
Instead of my mind with your words
I asked you to tell me something
Something about who you were on the inside
You said, *"I'm from Tennessee"*
As if that fucking meant shit about you
Your ex stalked me online for weeks
You said, *"She's harmless?"*
Your ex viciously lied about me
You said, *"She's harmless?"*
Your ex went crazy online
Writing all about her love for you
So… I told you all about it
You said, *"She's harmless?"*
Crazy girls like her are not harmless
Decent men shut crazy girls down
Before that crazy hurts anyone
But you allowed her crazy to flourish
You allowed her to continue
Causing havoc and chaos in my life
You see, you only wanted someone to fuck
Someone to call your *babe*

Bring Me Home

You never wanted anything more
Not with me anyway
You only want crazy girls
That you can manipulate and twist around
You were not able to handle my sanity
My logical lines of reasoning
That I sent in your direction
Whenever you did things that hurt me
When you got your feelings a little hurt
You decided that was the end of us
You're 38 and you have nothing longer than 3 years in dating
I should have known you would run
The second you realized
I was a real woman
And not a crazy little stalker girl
That you could manipulate with your games
I should have known better
But you told such sweet lies
Whenever you called me *babe*

Killing Silence

I wanted to keep writing about you
I thought maybe if I wrote more
Maybe you would feel my pain
Through my deeply written words
Then I realized I didn't want that
I didn't want you to feel this pain
Not like the pain I have been feeling
Your lies cut me deeper than you realize
Everything about you was fake
Right down to your artistic life
You are not a real artist
Artists have deep souls that feel deeply
Their beautiful souls shine through their artwork
Your soul is tainted with lies and manipulation

I wanted you to believe in you and your work
Because I wanted you in my life
I guess I just wanted the idea of you
I wanted the idea of a beautiful artist in my life
I know better now
You aren't a good idea
You are pure chaos and lies
Twisting a knife into the back of the universe
Expecting others to bend for you
When you refuse to even try for them
I wanted to keep writing about you
But you are no longer worth my time

ABOUT THE AUTHOR

EB Allen is a poet and artist from the Midwest. She finds that writing about her life gives her the escape that is necessary to move forward with all things in her life – sometimes it works and other times it is a band aid until the real healing has a chance to work its magic. You can find her other books Silent Kingdom, All of My Pieces and If I Love on amazon. Elle wants to deliver hope to those who feel lost in this world through her art. Even if she herself still feels completely misunderstood.